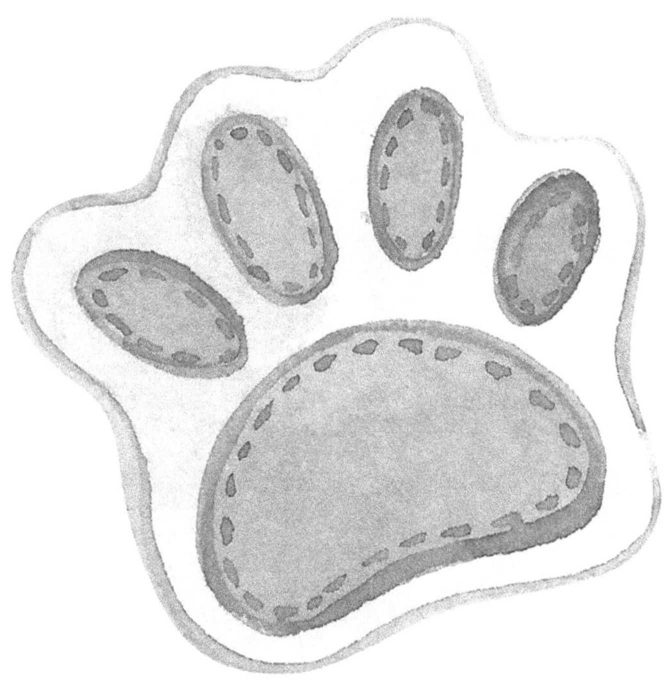

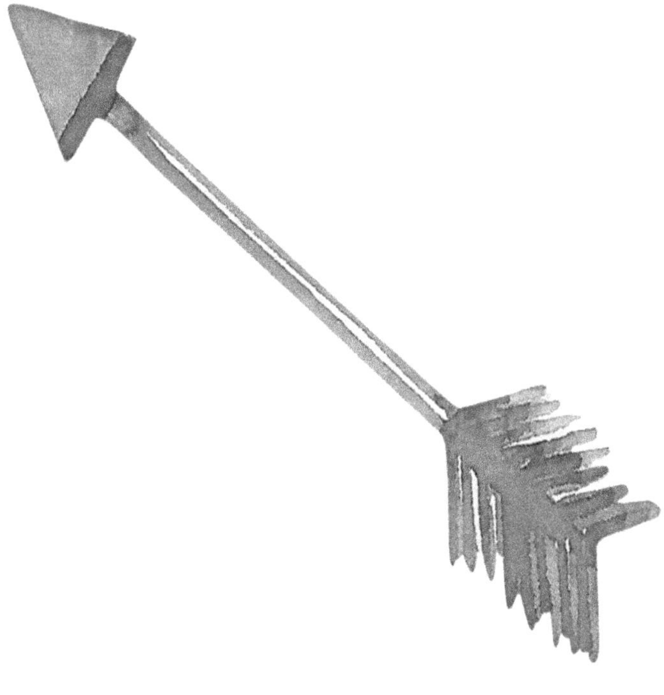

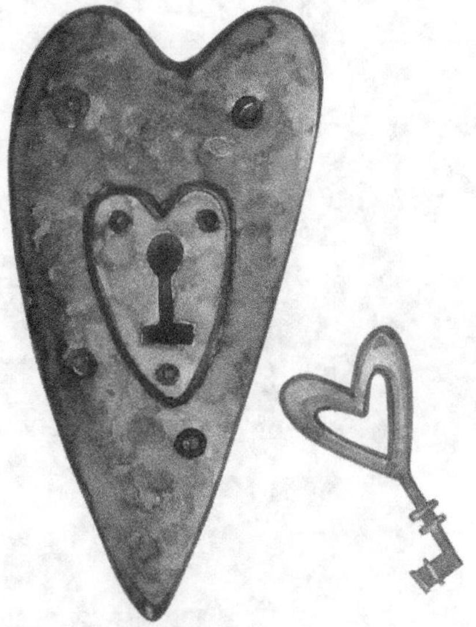

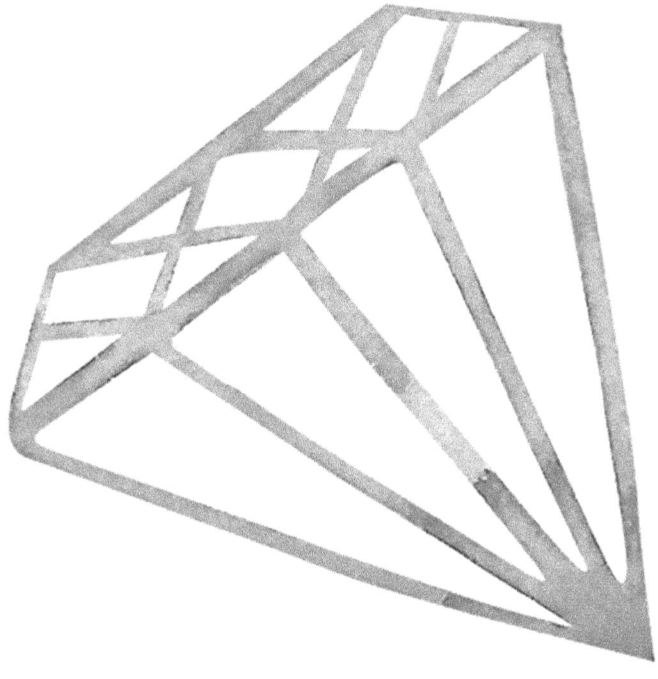

you
+
me
=
love

i love you

Love you

LOVE

you are loved

love is all you need

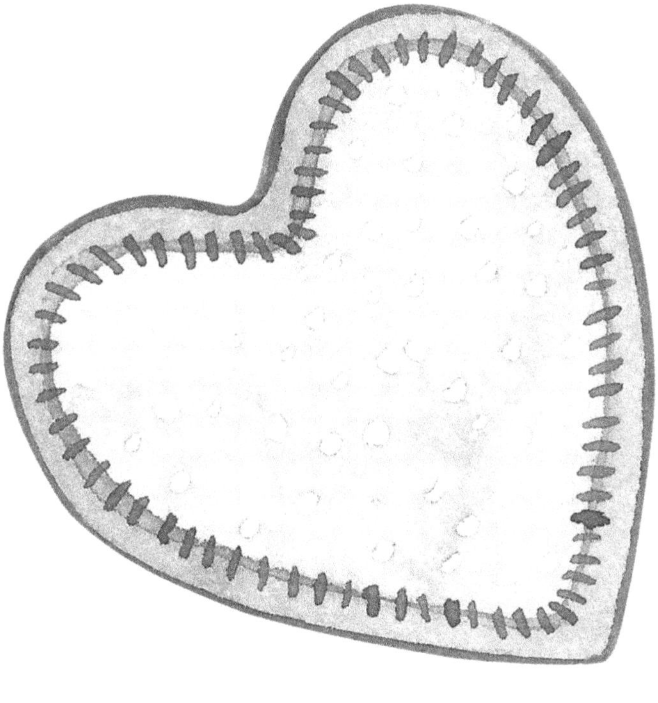

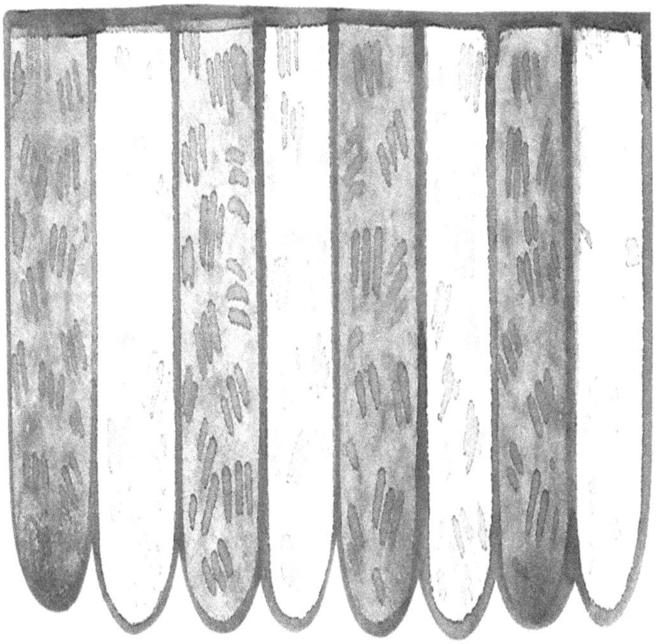

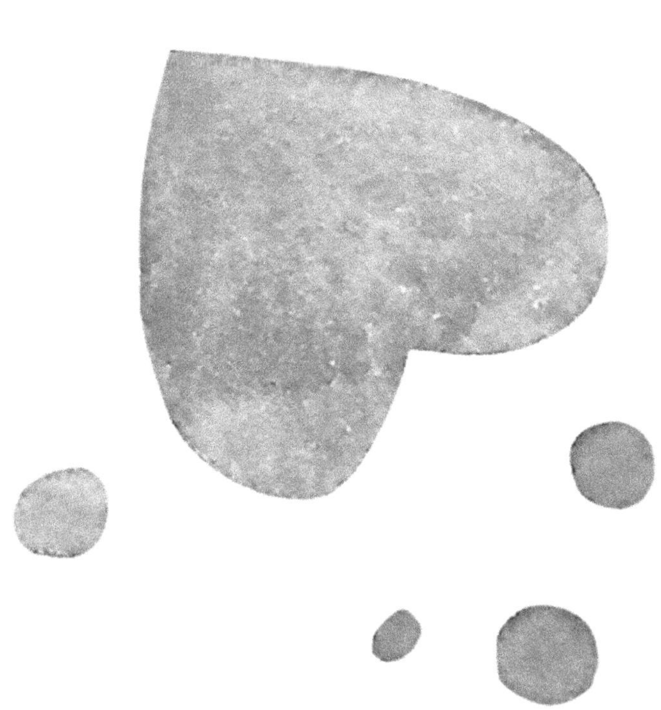

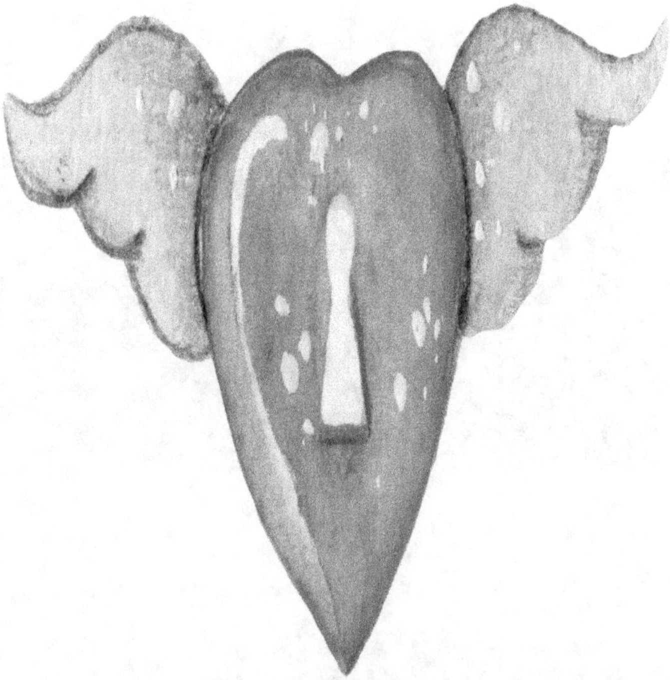

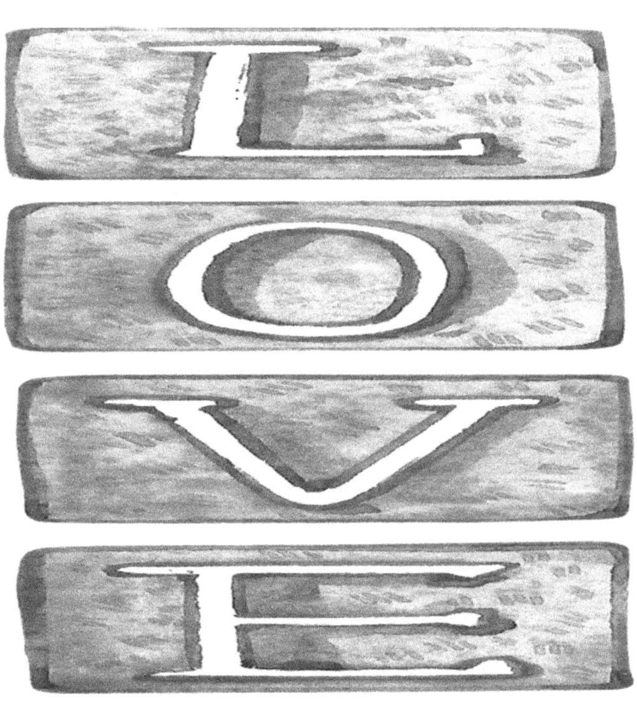
L
O
V
E

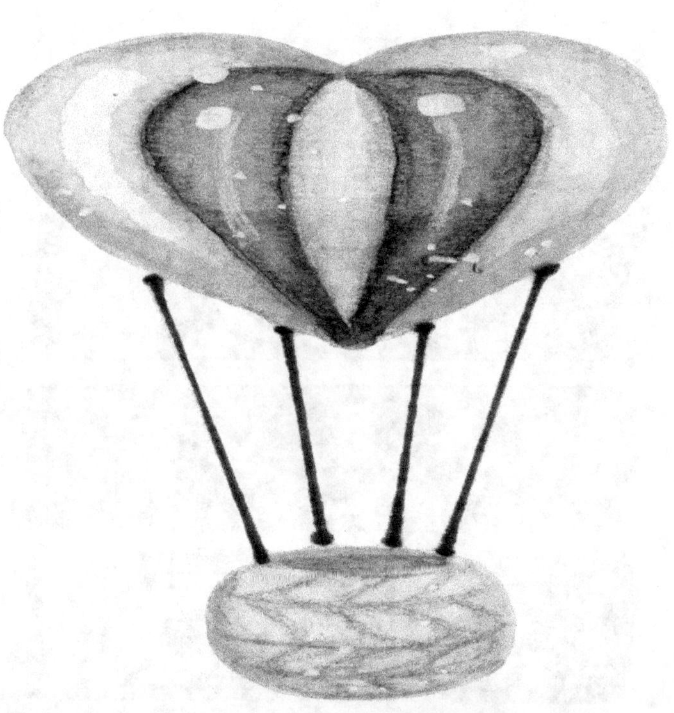

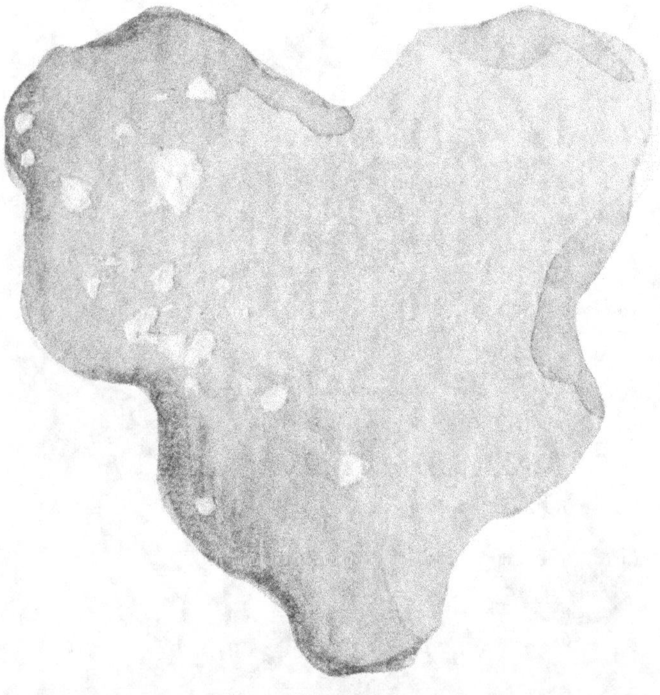

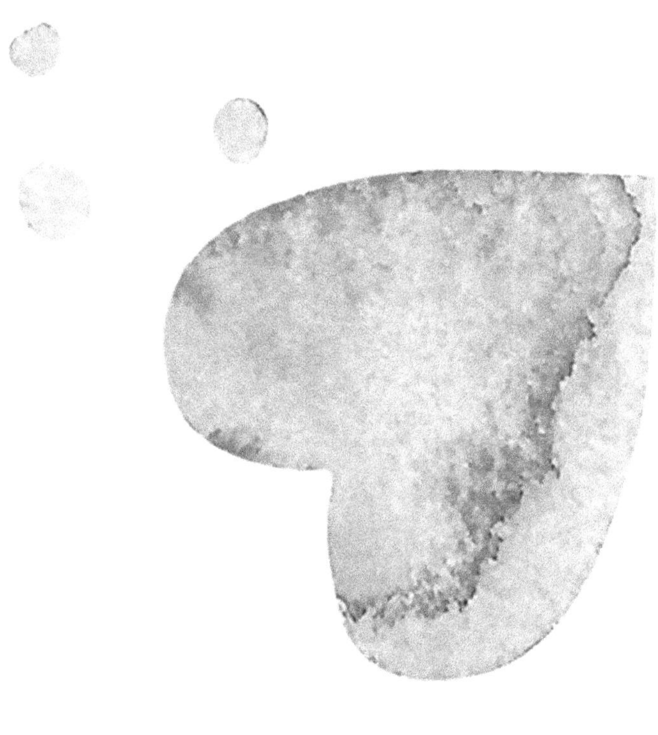

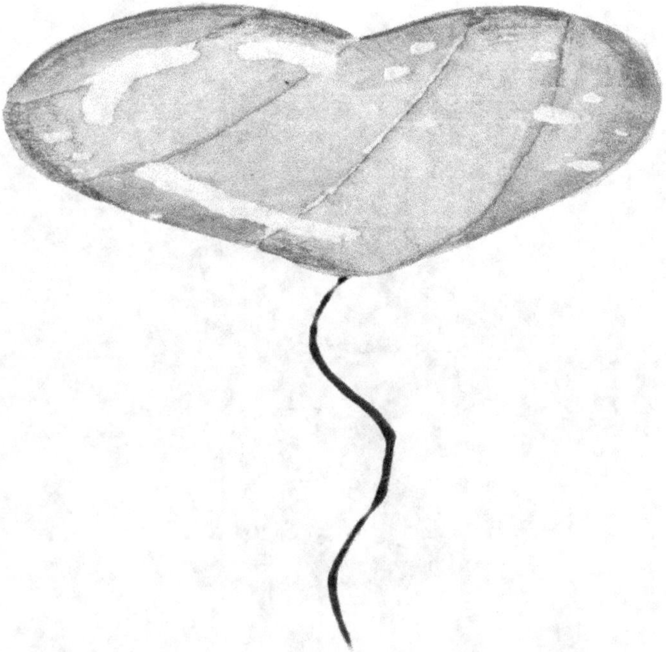

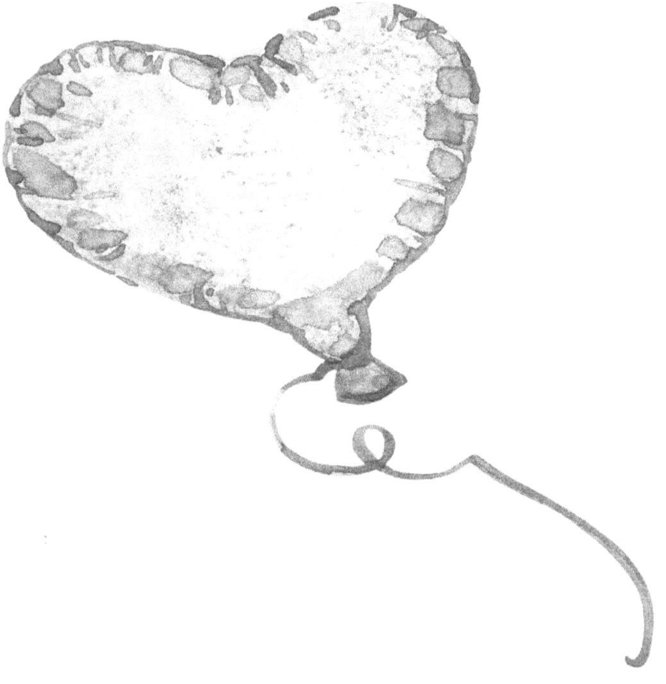

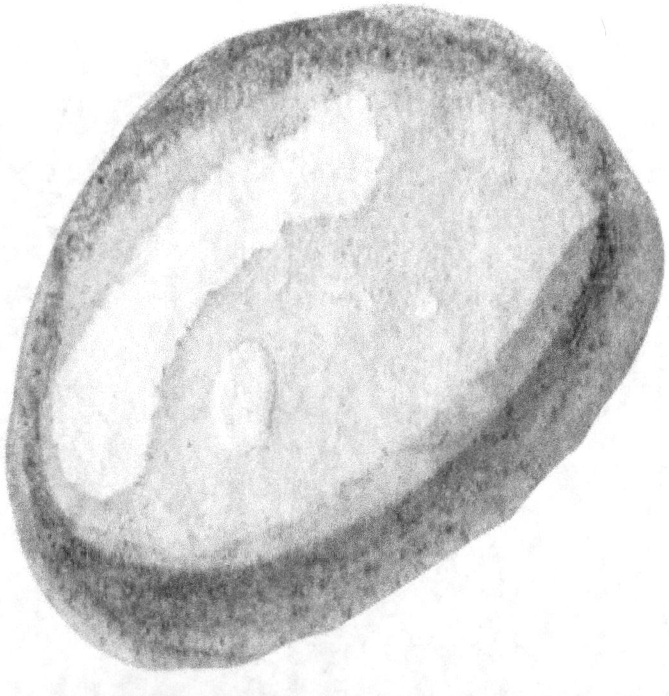

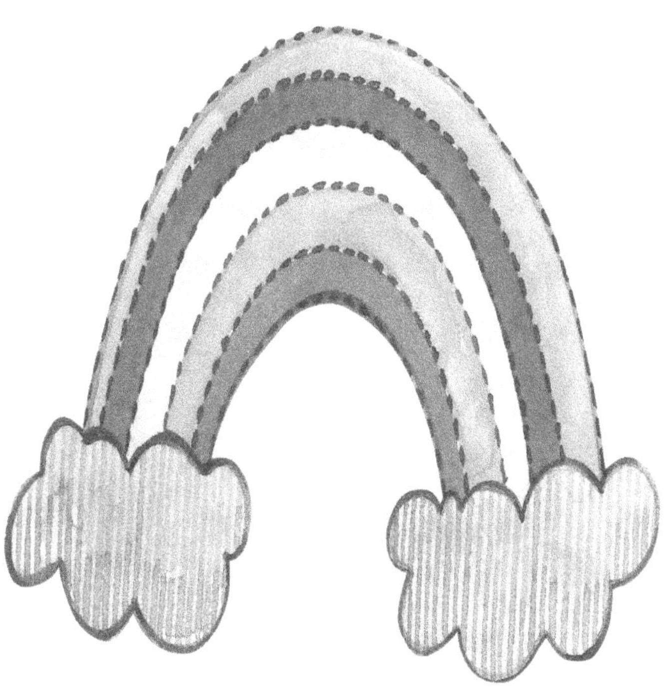

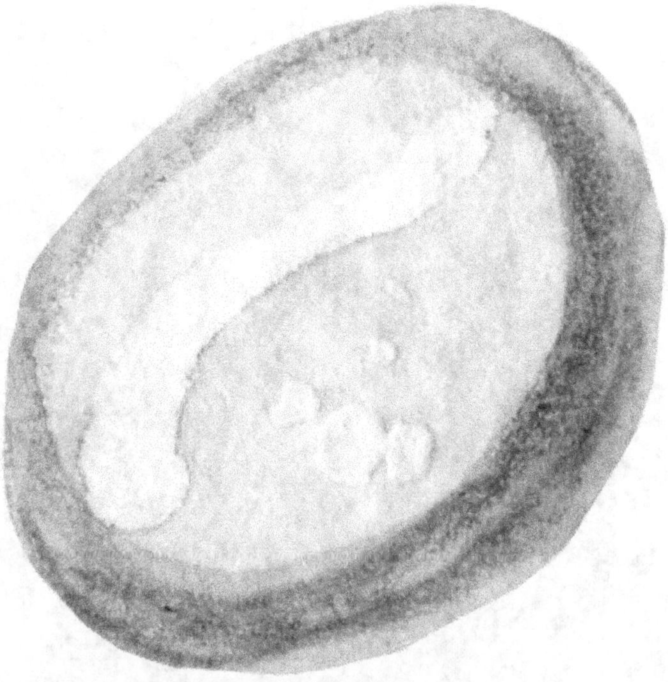

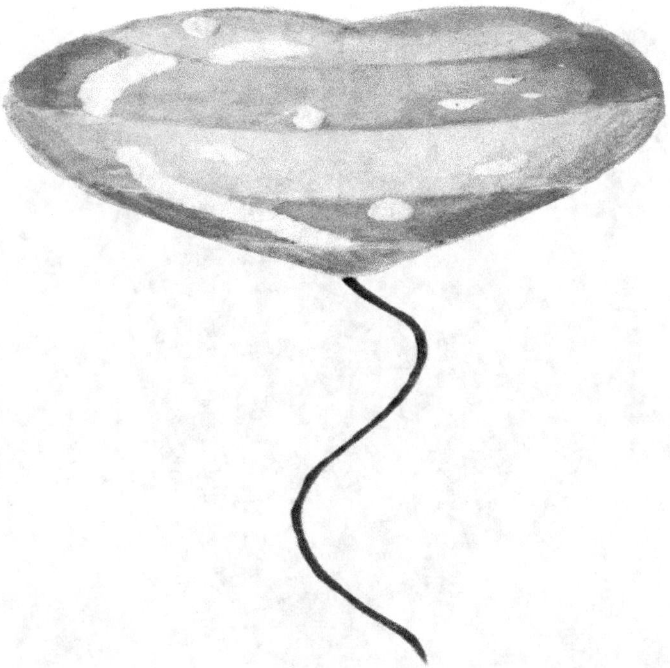

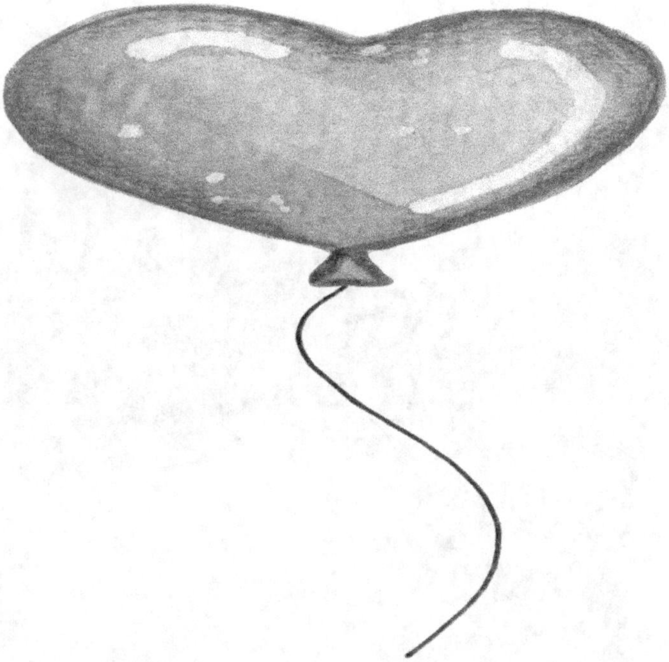

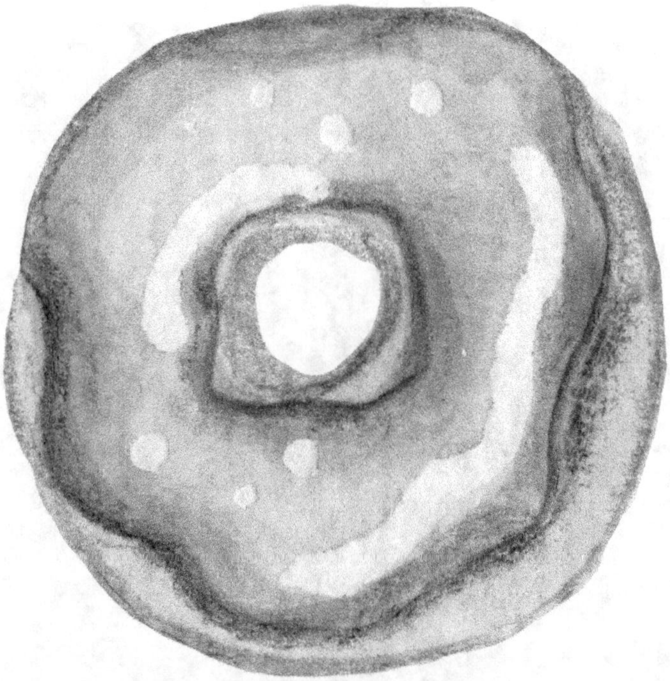

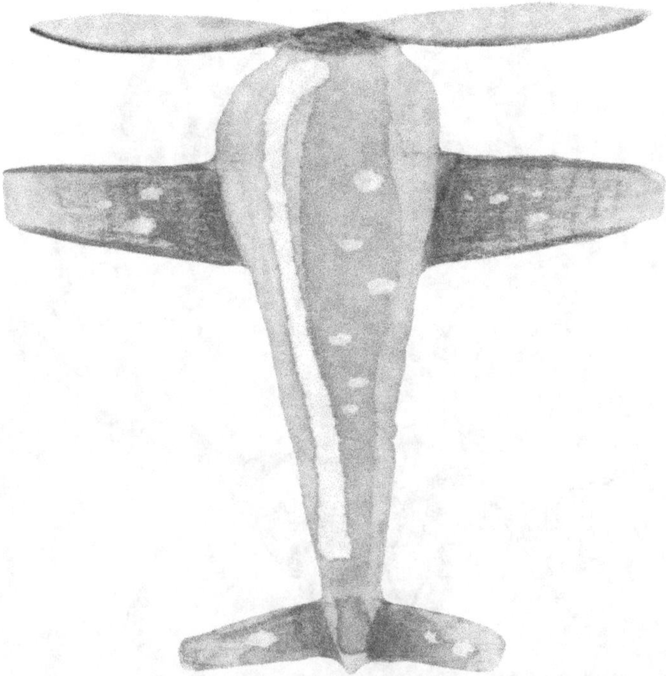

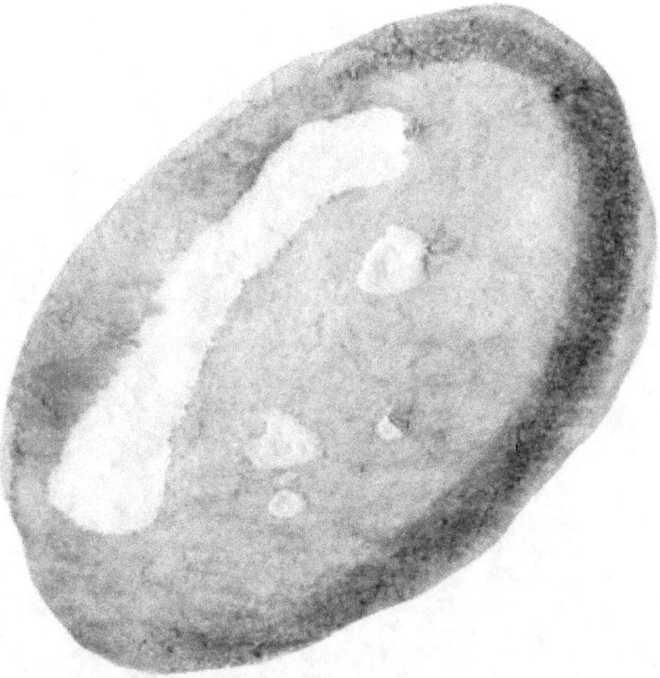

love

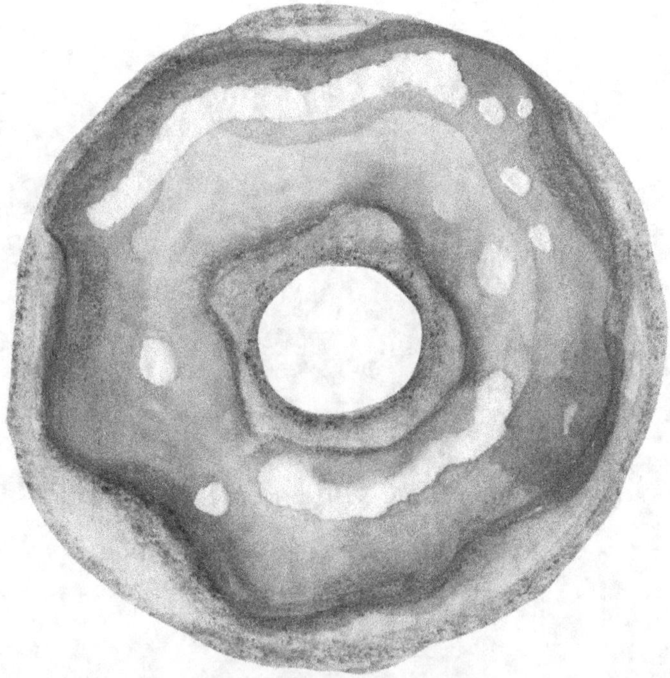

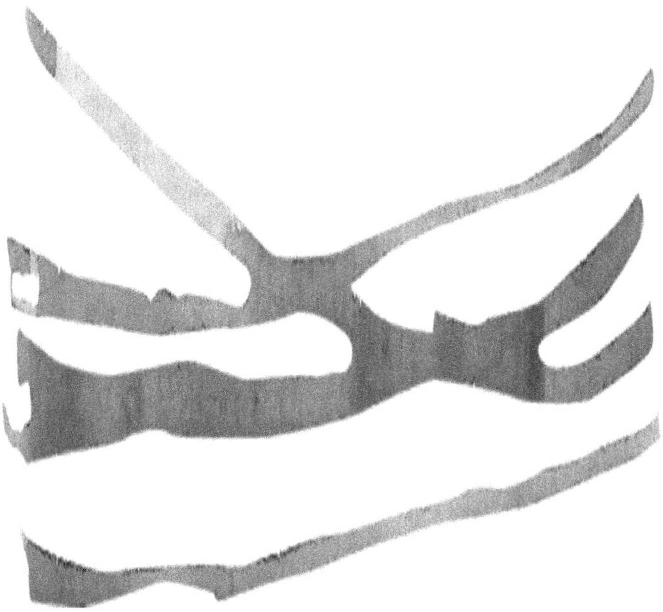

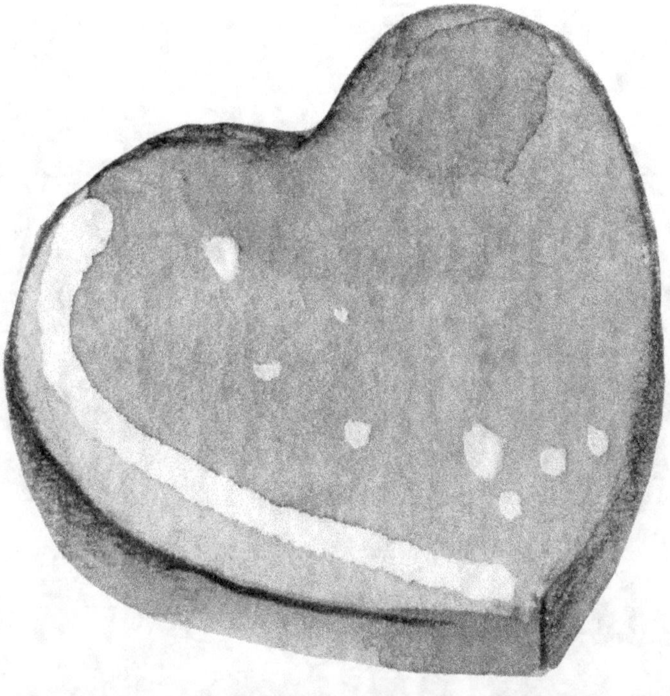

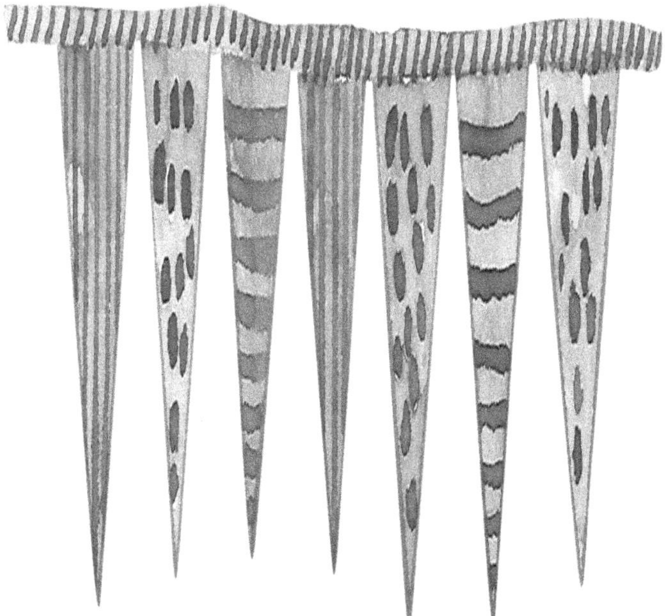

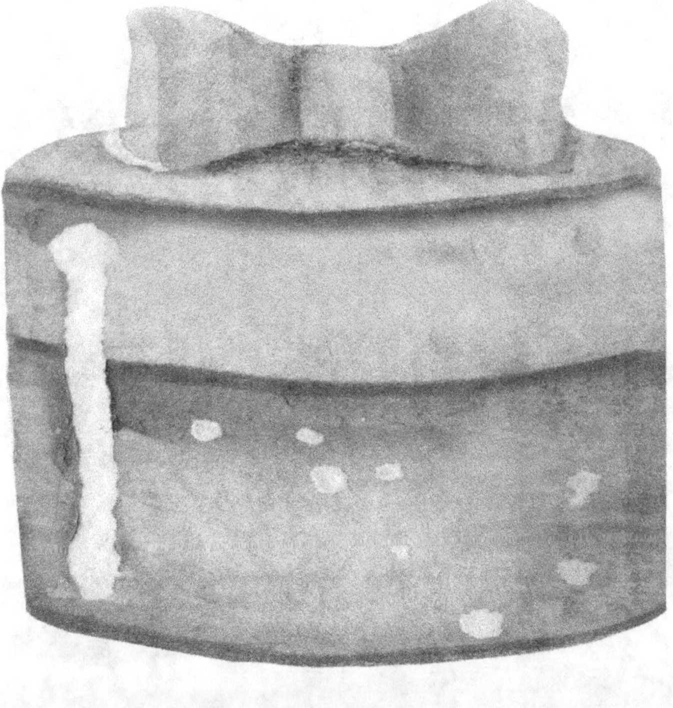

YAY

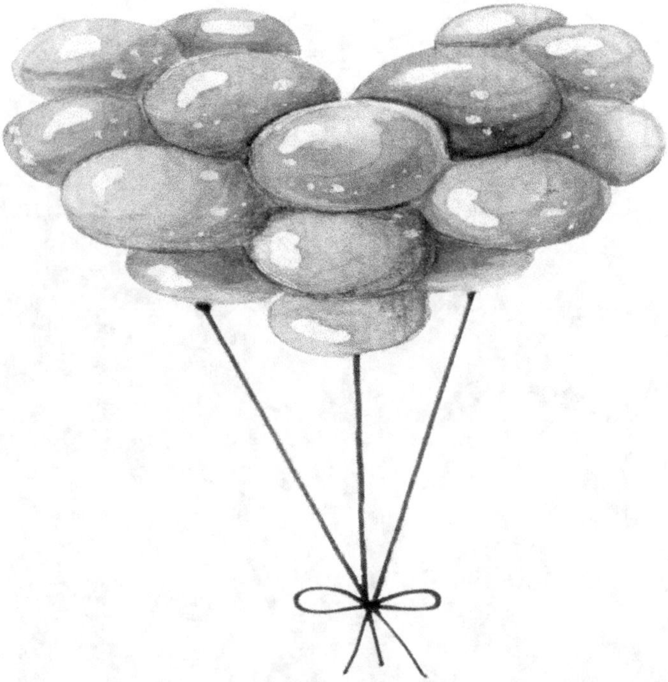

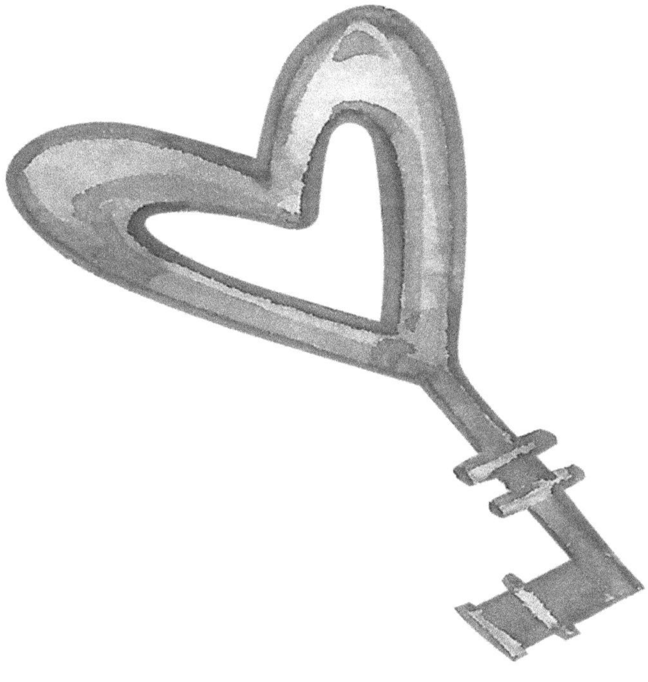

you
+
me
=
love

believe
IN
Love

love

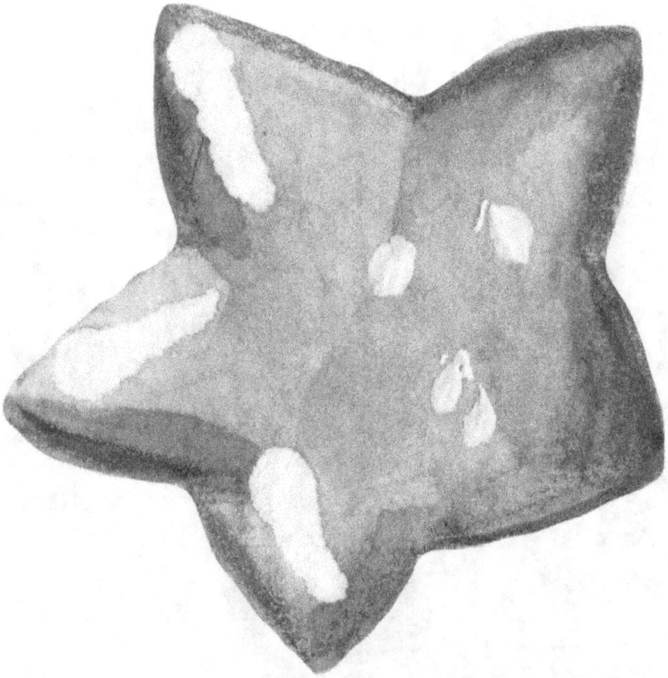

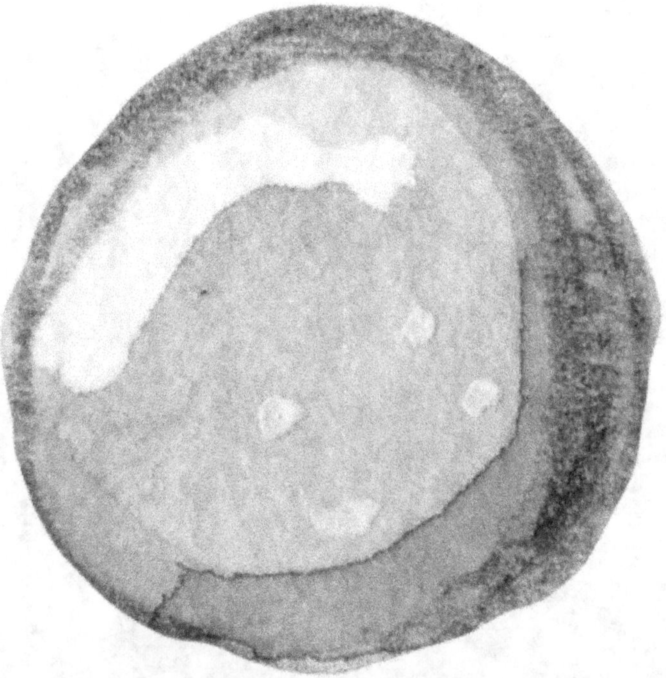

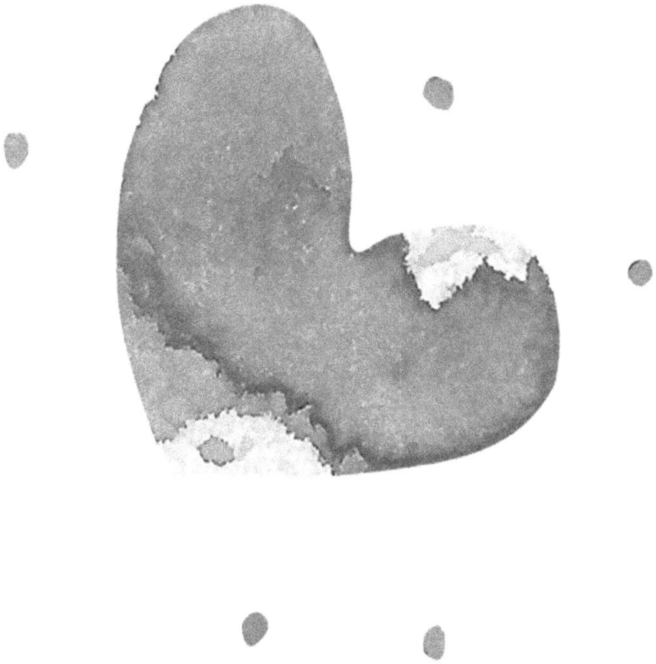

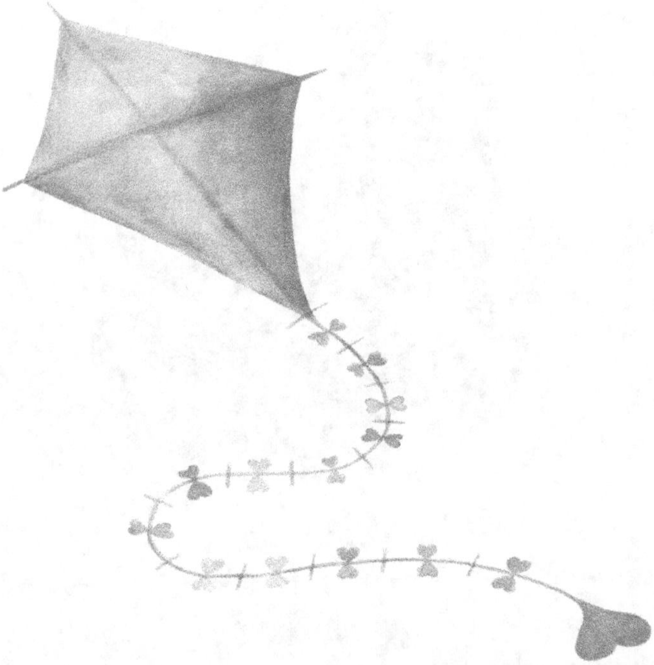

i love you

love you

Love

LOVE

Love

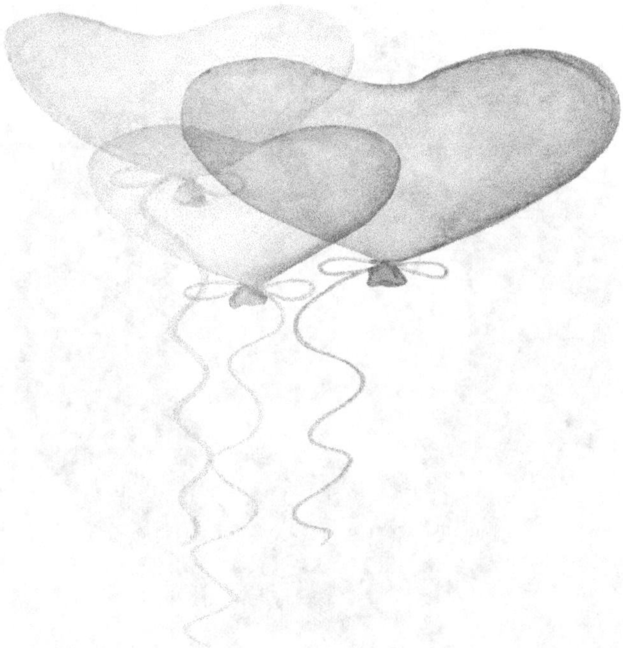

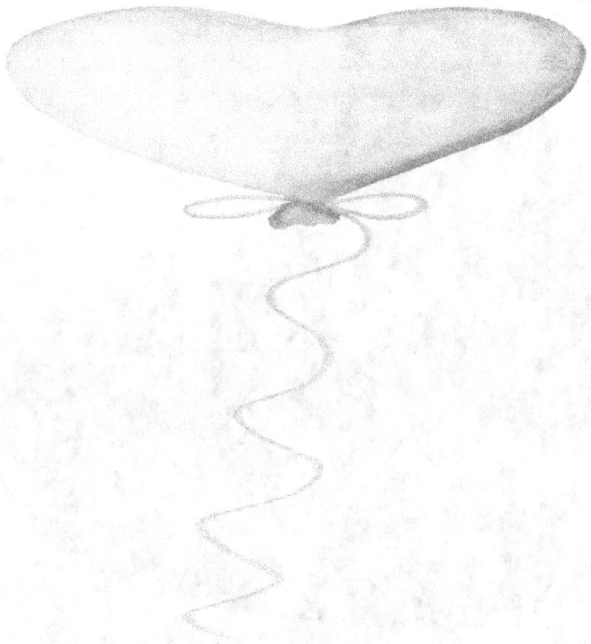

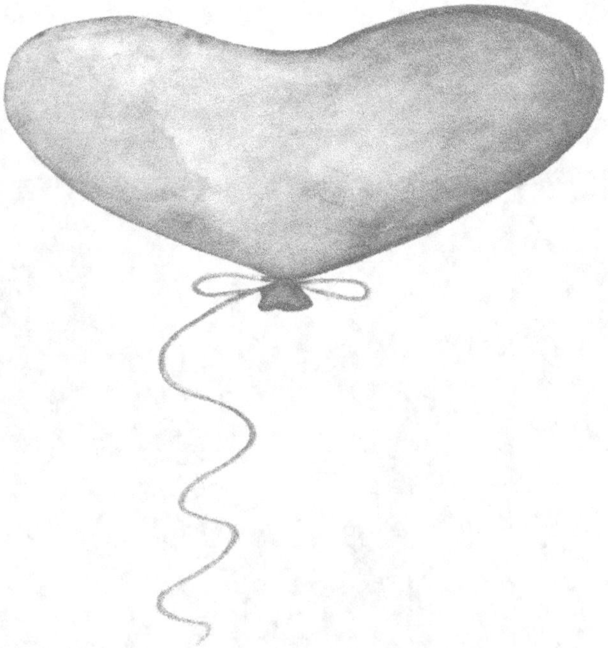

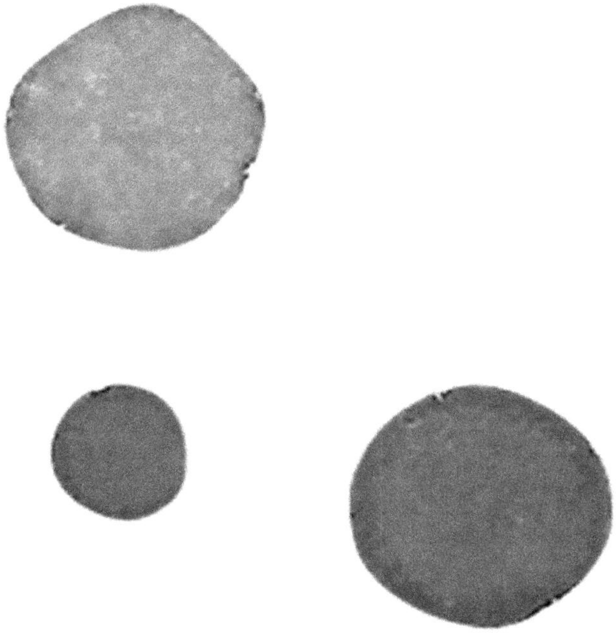

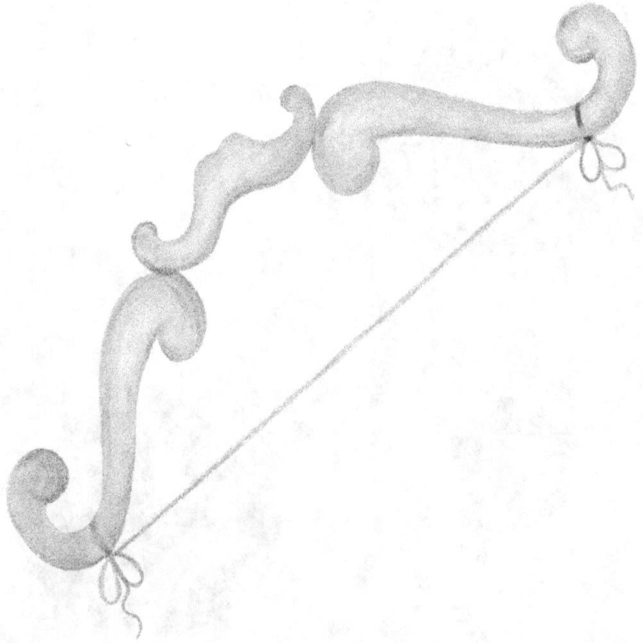

you are loved

love is all you need

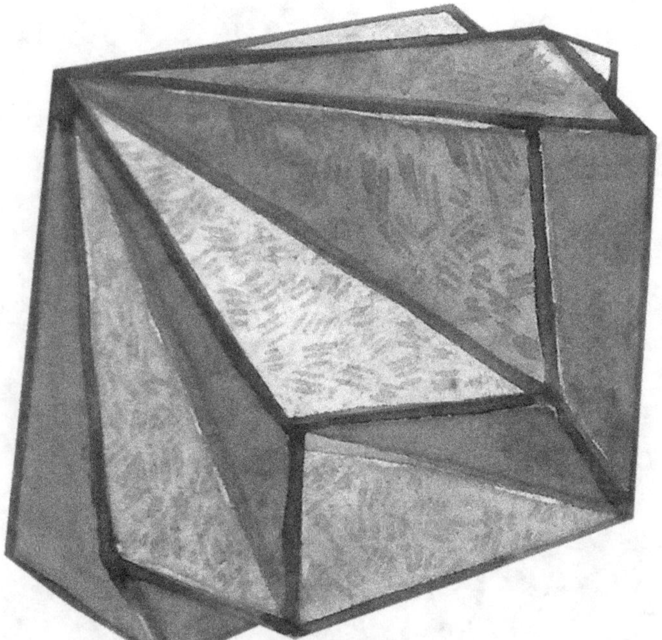

LOVE

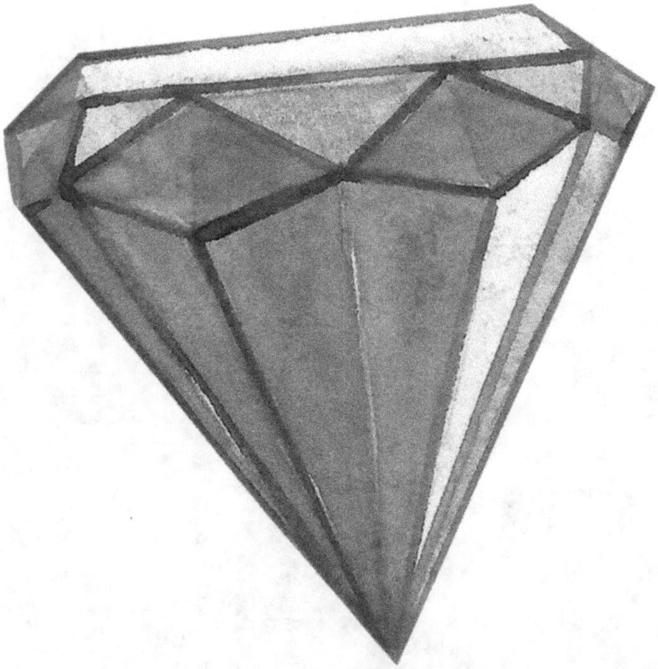

- Acts of Kindness Tracker -

- Acts of Kindness Tracker -

- Acts of Kindness Tracker -

Notes

Notes

Notes

www.ingramcontent.com/pod-product-compliance
Lightning Source LLC
LaVergne TN
LVHW060138080526
838202LV00049B/4016
* 9 7 8 3 3 4 7 0 3 0 0 5 3 *